■ Hello Boss,

I am Riaz Hussain A.K.A Trader Riaz. I am the Founder and CEO of Riaz Academy located in Bahria Town, Lahore, Pakistan. I have been trading for around a decade now. I blew up a number of my accounts and lost huge money just like every other trader. But then I learned a lot from my mistakes and built my own trading strategy from my experiences which eventually put me on track. I have been working on this same trading strategy for years now.

I learned that there must be some rules to follow if you really want to get something out of this financial market. Otherwise, you can never be a successful trader at all.

Yours,

Trader Riaz

Book Introduction:

There are mainly two reasons behind the failure of any trader:

1:- Analysis   2:- Rules

Why analysis becomes the reason of failure for a trader? It might be because he / she is not doing any analysis because he / she doesn't know how to do analysis before getting involved into any trade? The second possible reason could be that he is probably doing over analysis, considering unnecessary things before taking any trade.

Why rules become the reason of failure for a trader? It might be because he has no rules to follow before getting involved into any trade? The second possible reason could be that he is probably changing his rules most often. He doesn't give recommended time to his rules of trading before making new rules.

I have tried my best to give you as precise as possible and to the point knowledge of Analysis and Rules in this eBook that are necessary to make you a profitable trader.

I squeezed my whole knowledge in this eBook and I believe it will be more than enough for you to become a successful trader. Don't go for learning a lot of things.

Book Introduction:

Being a beginner trader, everyone feels that all we need to do is to focus on the chart. If price goes up we buy and if price goes down we sell. They believe this is the best way to make money. In fact this is not the case. Trading is not that easy.

If you are a trader and struggling to find good winning trades then this **Price Action Master Course** is for you because there could be some pieces of puzzle missing in your trading and you might get them from this eBook.

You can apply the **same concepts in Forex, Crypto or Stock trading** as this chart reading technique which you are going to learn in this eBook, can be easily implemented in any financial market.

I have tried my best to explain a step by step trading strategy to polish your trading skills. If you focus on the strategy mentioned in this course, you will definitely improve your winning percentage by the end of this course.

I believe this course will help you in minimizing your mistakes and becoming a successful trader in the end.

Good Luck!

Happy Trading

Price Action Master

Course Outline:

- Chapter 1: How to Identify Trend?

- Chapter 2: How to Identify Structure?

- Chapter 3: How to Take Entry & Exit?

- Chapter 4: 3-Step Trading Strategy

- Chapter 5: Gift Trading Strategy

Index Page 1:

Index Page 2:

Swing Levels:

- What is a Swing Level?

- How to identify a perfect Swing Level?

- Types of Swing Levels:

    - Major Swing Level

    - Minor Swing Level

Swing Levels:

■ What is a Swing Level?

Price moves and changes direction numerous times on the chart during a particular time frame in which you are observing the price action or behavior. So, every point on the chart from where the price changes its direction, is considered a swing level.

For example: in the illustration below, every point which has been circled is actually a Swing Level.

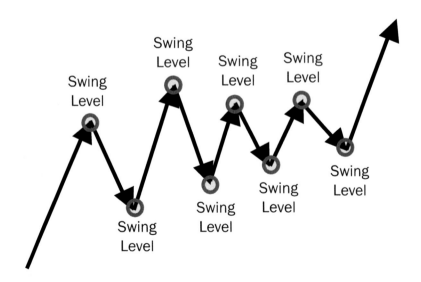

Swing Levels:

■ **How to Identify a Perfect Swing Level?**

A swing level can be of two different types:

– Swing High

- Every top of a price move is considered a swing high; if

- A high that has at least two candles including wicks below on both left and right side

– Swing Low

- Every bottom of a price move is considered a swing low; if

- A low that has at least two candles including wicks above on both left and right side

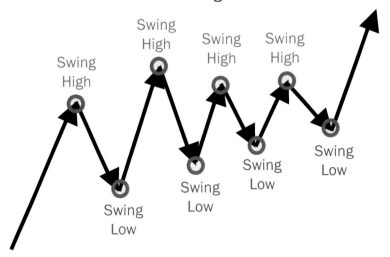

Swing Levels:

■ How to Identify a Perfect Swing Level?

Examples of a perfect swing level:

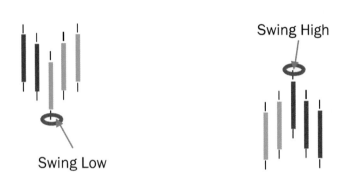

Swing Low

Swing High

Swing High

Swing Low

Swing Levels:

■ Types of Swing Levels:

There are two types of swing levels.

– Major Swing Level

  ■ Major swing levels are actually the extreme points of any move

– Minor Swing Level

  ■ Minor swing levels are formed within the range of a major swing high and major swing low

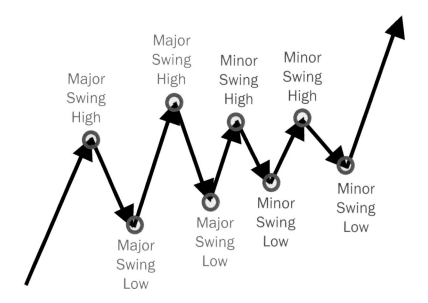

Swing Levels:

■ Major Swing Level:

- Major swing levels are formed at the top and bottom of any big impulsive or corrective moves.

- These levels are generally called Higher Highs, Higher Lows, Lower Highs or Lower Lows.

- Major swing levels are considered the only tradable points in Price Action Trading Strategies.

- We only need to focus on major swing levels during our trading plans.

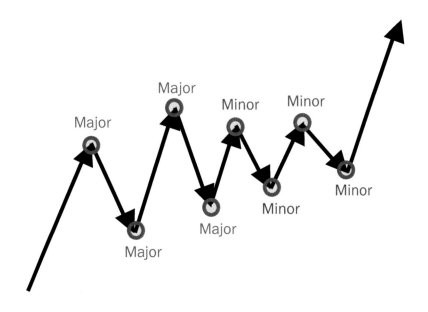

Swing Levels:

■ Minor Swing Level:

- – Minor swing levels are formed within the range of two major swing levels.
- – One of these two major swing levels must be a major swing high and second must be a major swing low.
- – Minor swing levels are not considered the tradable points in Price Action Trading Strategies.
- – We don't consider minor swing levels during our trading plans.

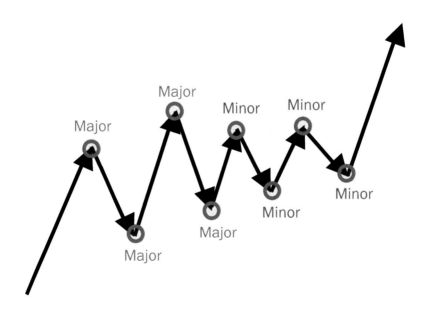

Swing Levels:

■ **Example on Chart:**

– Examples of Major & Minor Swing Levels on the Chart

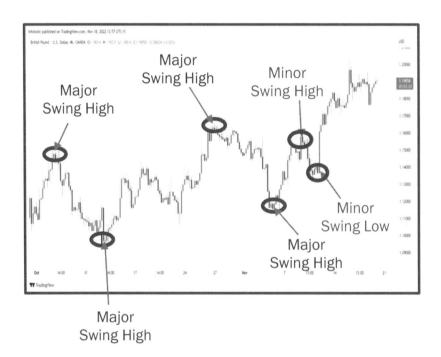

Trends:

- What is a Trend?

- Types of Trends:

    - Uptrend

    - Downtrend

    - Sideways Trend / Range-bound Trend

Trends:

■ What is a Trend?

- A trend is a tendency for prices to move in a particular direction over a period of time.

- Trends can be upward, downward and even sideways.

- Whenever the price completes 1, 2 & 3 move in any direction, we consider it an uptrend or downtrend.

- 1, 2 & 3 move in a bigger time frame (4H & above) is more reliable then the 1, 2 & 3 move we find in lower time frames.

- So, we should not consider 1, 2 & 3 moves in lower time frames to plan our trades.

| Uptrend | Sideways Trend | Downtrend |

Trends:

■ What is an Uptrend?

- Whenever the price completes 1, 2 & 3 move in upward direction, we consider it an uptrend.

- As long as the price is making new higher highs and highering its lows, the instrument is considered to be in an uptrend (see example 1 on next slide).

- Only major swing highs qualify as the higher highs and likewise, only major swing lows qualify as the higher low of an uptrend.

- We do not mark any swing low as a new higher low unless we have a new higher high on the chart.

- Price must make a new higher high first then we spot the lowest swing level made by the price after previous higher high. This lowest swing low wins as our new higher low for the uptrend (see example 2 on next slide).

- The price is considered to be in an uptrend as long as the price is trading above the most recent higher low.

- Whenever the price breaks & closes below the most recent higher low of an uptrend, we consider it as one of the early signs of trend reversal.

Trends:

■ **Uptrend Examples:**

– Examples of an uptrend on chart:

■ See the price is making new higher highs and also highering its lows.

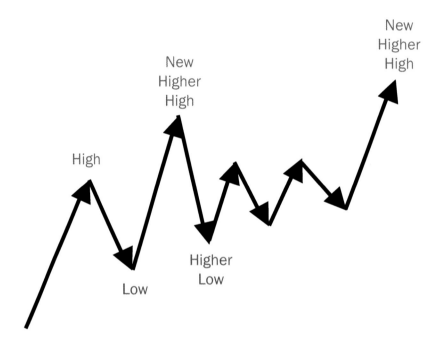

Example 1:

Trends:

■ **Uptrend Example:**

   – Example of an uptrend on chart:

      ■ See we selected the lowest swing low as our new higher low after we see the price made new higher high.

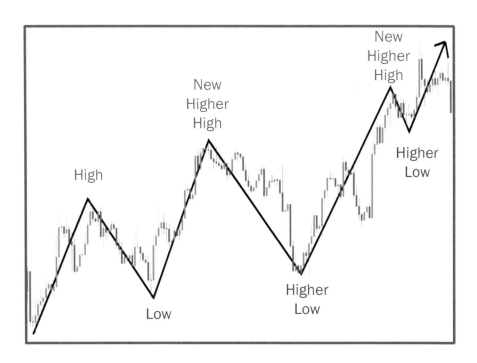

Example 2:

Trends:

■ **What is a Valid Breakout in an Uptrend?**

– Whenever the price breaks and closes above the previous higher high and tries to make a new higher high, we consider it a valid breakout only if we get two candles closing above the highest wick of the previous higher high (see example below)

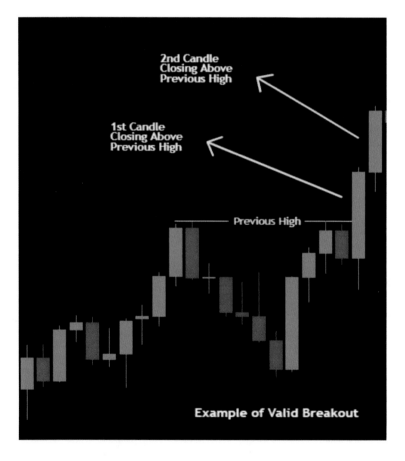

Trends:

■ **What is a Valid Breakout in an Uptrend?**

– Some times we see that 1st candle closes above the previous higher high but then price goes into consolidation and then after making few candles price closes above the wick of 1st candle. It also qualifies as a valid breakout(see example below)

Trends:

■ What is a Downtrend?

- Whenever the price completes 1, 2 & 3 move in downward direction, we consider it a downtrend.

- As long as the price is making new lower lows and lowering its highs, the instrument is considered to be in a downtrend (see example 1 on next slide).

- Only major swing highs qualify as the lower highs and likewise, only major swing lows qualify as the lower low of an downtrend.

- We do not mark any swing high as a new lower high unless we have a new lower low on the chart.

- Price must make a new lower low first then we spot the highest swing level made by the price after previous lower low. This highest swing high wins as our new lower high for the downtrend (see example 2 on next slide).

- The price is considered to be in a downtrend as long as the price is trading below the most recent lower high.

- Whenever the price breaks & closes above the most recent lower high of a downtrend, we consider it as one of the early signs of trend reversal.

Trends:

■ **Downtrend Example:**

　– Example of a downtrend on chart:

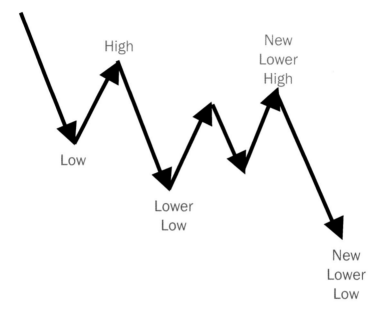

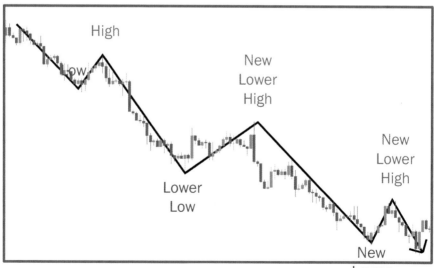

Trends:

■ **What is a Valid Breakout in an Downtrend?**

– Whenever the price breaks and closes below the previous lower low and tries to make a new lower low, we consider it a valid breakout only if we get two candles closing above the lowest wick of the previous lower low (see example below)

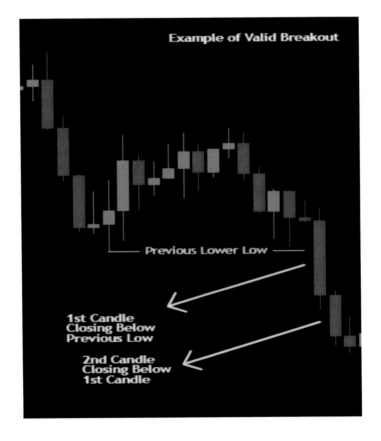

Trends:

■ What is a Valid Breakout in an Downtrend?

– Some times we see that 1st candle closes below the previous lower low but then price goes into consolidation and then after making few candles price closes below the wick of 1st candle. It also qualifies as a valid breakout(see example below)

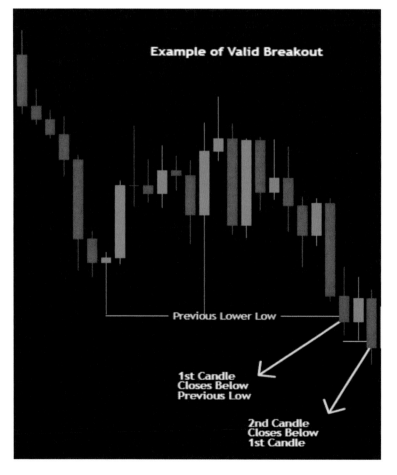

Example of Valid Breakout

Previous Lower Low

1st Candle
Closes Below
Previous Low

2nd Candle
Closes Below
1st Candle

https://www.youtube.com/@TraderRiaz

Trends:

■ What is a Sideways Trend?

- Whenever the price completes 1, 2, 3 & 4 move in a range during an uptrend or a downtrend, that particular phase of the price is considered a sideways trend.

- Or you can say that If the price is unable to make new highs or lows, the instrument is considered to be in a sideways trend.

- As long as the price doesn't break the high or low of that range, we consider the price is no trend, range-bound or in a sideways trend.

- Sideways trend is never considered to be a trading opportunity so we must avoid trading when we see the price is trading sideways.

- Whenever the price breaks & closes above or below the high or low of this sideways trend, it might becomes an indication of an uptrend or downtrend.

Trends:

■ **Sideways Trend Example:**

– Example of a sideways trend on chart:

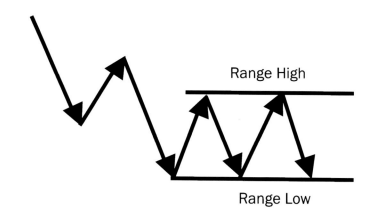

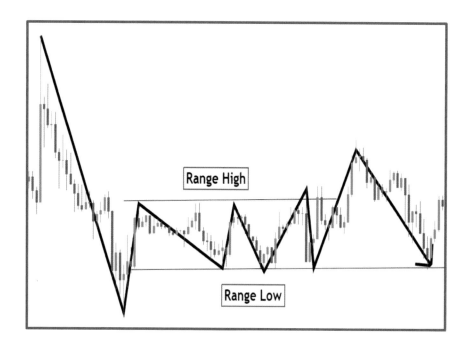

Pullbacks:

- What is a Pullback?

- Types of Pullbacks:

    - Short Pullback

    - Medium Pullback

    - Deep Pullback

Pullbacks:

■ What is a Pullback?

– A pullback is a temporary pause in an asset's overall trend. It is generally recognized as a downward move in an uptrend or an upward move in a downtrend.

– Whenever the price takes turn to the downward direction during an uptrend, it might be considered a pullback. Likewise whenever the price takes turn to the upward direction during a downtrend, it might be considered a pullback.

– Generally, a pullback is a valid pullback only if it consists on at least two candles.

– A single candle pullback is also valid but if:

■ It takes the low of the last green or red candle and then continue upward (in case of an uptrend); or

■ It takes the high of the last red or green candle and then continue downward (in case of a downtrend)

Pullbacks:

■ Short Pullback (SP):

- A short pullback is a pullback that doesn't come back to retest previous higher high (in uptrend) or previous lower low (in downtrend) and then continue its trend.

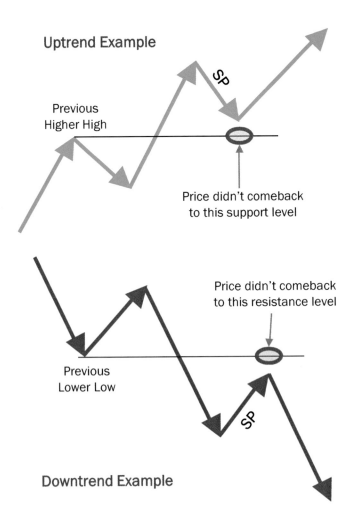

Uptrend Example

SP

Previous Higher High

Price didn't comeback to this support level

Price didn't comeback to this resistance level

Previous Lower Low

SP

Downtrend Example

Pullbacks:

■ **Medium Pullback (MP):**

- A medium pullback is a pullback that comes back to
  retest previous higher high (in uptrend) or previous
  lower low (in downtrend) and then continue its trend.

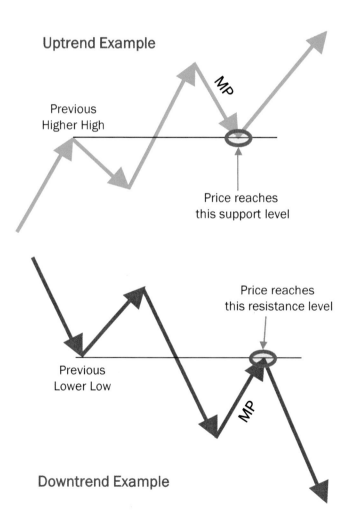

Uptrend Example

Previous
Higher High

MP

Price reaches
this support level

Price reaches
this resistance level

Previous
Lower Low

MP

Downtrend Example

Pullbacks:

■ Deep Pullback (DP):

  – A deep pullback is a pullback that comes deep to the previous lower high (in downtrend) or previous higher low (in uptrend) and then continue its trend.

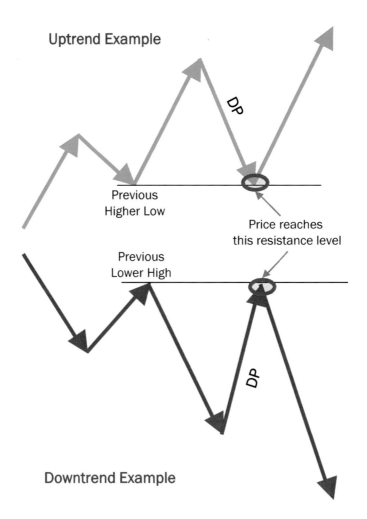

Structures:

- What is Support & Resistance?

- Types of Support:

    – Direct Support

    – Indirect Support

- Types of Resistance:

    – Direct Resistance

    – Indirect Resistance

Support:

■ What is a Support Level?

- A support level is a price zone on the chart where traders think they might get a BUY or LONG trade off of.

- Always try to find support nearest to the area where price is trading at the moment and then draw a horizontal line there to see if this level has been respected by the price multiple times or not.

- A support level becomes very strong if it has been tested / respected by the price multiple times (at least two times).

For Example:

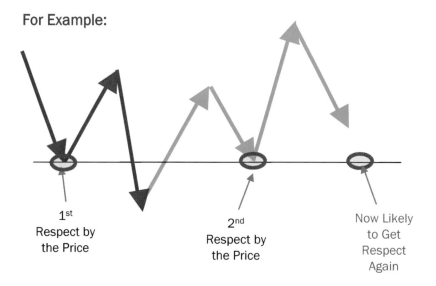

1st
Respect by
the Price

2nd
Respect by
the Price

Now Likely
to Get
Respect
Again

Support:

■ Types of Support Level:

   – Support Level is of two types:

      ■ Direct Support

        – Any support area on the chart which has not been touched by the price.

      ■ In-Direct Support

        – Any support area on the chart which is made after seeing through the price.

   – Let's discuss direct and in-direct support examples in the next slides.

Support:

■ Example 1 of In-Direct Support Level:

- – Let suppose current trend is up and when price breaks its previous high after taking a pullback, it becomes immediate support for the price.

- – This is the area where we might get our BUY / LONG trade opportunity because price is likely to respect this level as a support for the price.

Example 1 (Uptrend):

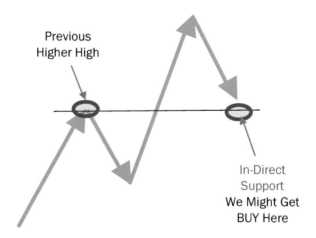

Previous Higher High

In-Direct Support We Might Get BUY Here

Support:

■ Example 2 of In-Direct Support Level:

- Let suppose current trend is down but then price breaks and closes above the most recent lower high.

- This was a resistance but after breaking and closing above this level, it becomes support to the price and we might get a BUY / LONG trade off of same level only if we get any entry reason there.

- There are high chances that price is likely to respect this level as a support for the price.

Example 2 (Downtrend Reversal):

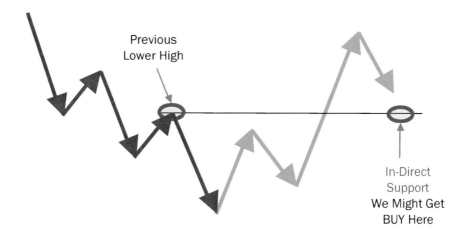

Support:

■ Example 1 of Direct Support Level:

- Let suppose current trend is up. Price didn't give any respect to in-direct support level and took a deep pullback to higher low. Now this higher low becomes support to the price and we might get a BUY / LONG trade off of same level only if we get any entry reason there.

- As long as the price is trading above higher low in this case, we are still in an uptrend. If price breaks and closes below this higher low level, then we might have a trend reversal opportunity.

- There are high chances that price is likely to respect this level as a support for the price because this is the last chance for the buyers to retain price in uptrend.

Support:

■ **Example 1 of Direct Support Level:**

Example 3 (Uptrend):

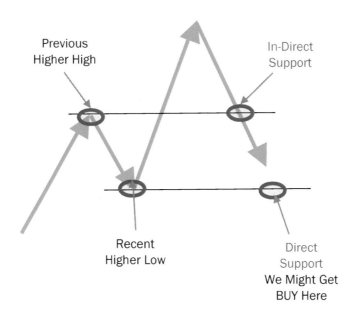

Previous
Higher High

In-Direct
Support

Recent
Higher Low

Direct
Support
We Might Get
BUY Here

Support:

■ **Example 2 of Direct Support Level:**

- Let suppose current trend is down but when price approaches to any higher low of previous uptrend, it might work as a strong support for the price and we might get a BUY / LONG trade off of same level only if we get any entry reason there.

- As this is still a fresh support level for the price therefore, there are high chances that price is likely to respect this level as a support level.

- Although we are still in a downtrend but these are the levels where we might expect trend reversal opportunities.

Support:

■ **Example 2 of Direct Support Level:**

Example 4 (Downtrend):

Resistance:

■ What is a Resistance Level?

- A resistance level is a price zone on the chart where traders think they might get a SELL or SHORT trade off of.

- Always try to find resistance nearest to the area where price is trading at the moment and then draw a horizontal line there to see if this level has been respected by the price multiple times or not.

- A resistance level becomes very strong if it has been tested / respected by the price multiple times (at least two times).

For Example:

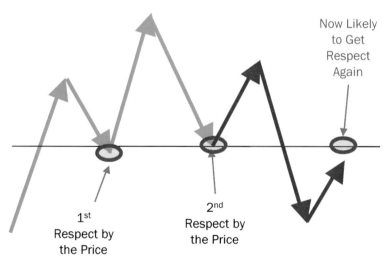

Resistance:

■ **Types of Resistance Level:**

– Resistance Level is of two types:

■ **Direct Resistance**

– Any resistance area on the chart which has not been touched by the price.

■ **In-Direct Resistance**

– Any resistance area on the chart which is made after seeing through the price.

– Let's discuss direct and in-direct resistance examples in the next slides.

Resistance:

■ **Example 1 of In-Direct Resistance Level:**

- Let suppose current trend is down and when price breaks its previous low after taking a pullback, it becomes immediate resistance for the price.

- This is the area where we might get our SELL / SHORT trade opportunity because price is likely to respect this level as a resistance for the price.

Example 1 (Downtrend):

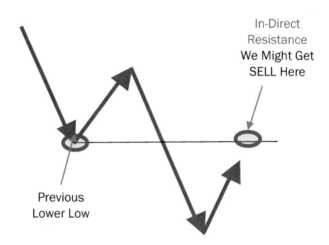

Resistance:

■ **Example 2 of In-Direct Resistance Level:**

- Let suppose current trend is up but then price breaks and closes below the most recent higher low.

- This was a support level but after breaking and closing below this level, it becomes immediate resistance to the price and we might get a SELL / SHORT trade off of same level only if we get any entry reason there.

- There are high chances that price is likely to respect this level as a resistance for the price.

Resistance:

■ **Example 2 of In-Direct Resistance Level:**

Example 2 (Uptrend Reversal):

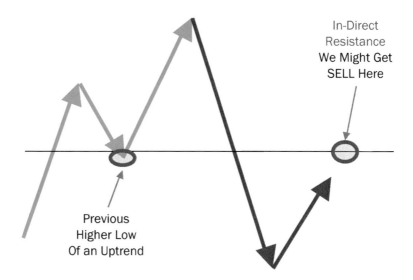

In-Direct
Resistance
We Might Get
SELL Here

Previous
Higher Low
Of an Uptrend

Resistance:

■ **Example 1 of Direct Resistance Level:**

– Let suppose current trend is down. Price didn't give any respect to in-direct resistance level and took a deep pullback to lower high. Now this lower high becomes resistance to the price and we might get a SELL / SHORT trade off of same level only if we get any entry reason there.

– As long as the price is trading below lower high in this case, we are still in a downtrend. If price breaks and closes above this lower high, then we might have a trend reversal opportunity.

– There are high chances that price is likely to respect this level as a resistance for the price because this is the last chance for the sellers to retain price in downtrend.

Resistance:

■ **Example 1 of Direct Resistance Level:**

Example 3 (Downtrend):

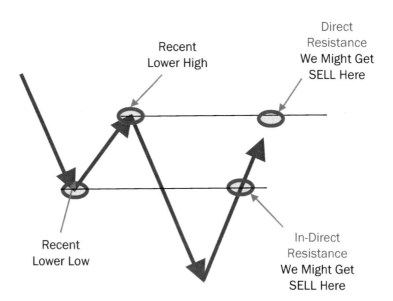

Direct
Resistance
We Might Get
SELL Here

Recent
Lower High

In-Direct
Resistance
We Might Get
SELL Here

Recent
Lower Low

Resistance:

■ **Example 2 of Direct Resistance Level:**

    – Let suppose current trend is up but when price approaches to any lower high of previous downtrend, it might work as a strong resistance for the price and we might get a SELL / SHORT trade off of same level only if we get any entry reason there.

    – As this is still a fresh resistance level for the price therefore, there are high chances that price is likely to respect this level as a resistance level.

    – Although we are still in an uptrend but these are the levels where we might expect trend reversal opportunities.

Resistance:

■ Example 2 of Direct Resistance Level:

Example 4 (Uptrend):

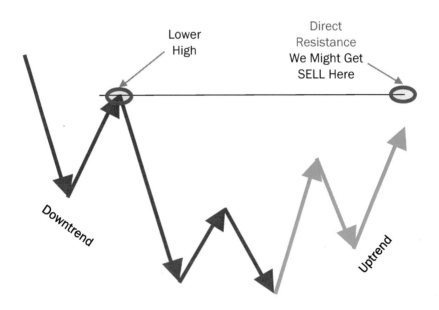

Entry Zone:

- ■ What is an Entry Zone?

- ■ How to Draw an Entry Zone?

■ What is an Entry Zone?

– An entry zone is actually the last red or green candle of any Move 1 in a downtrend or uptrend respectively based on our support or resistance levels.

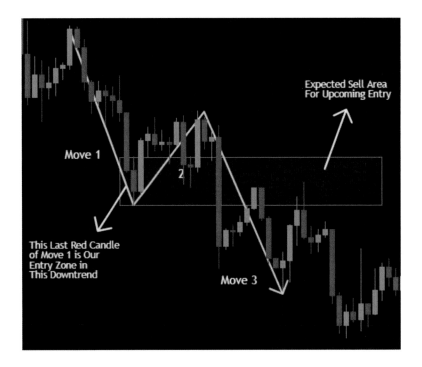

Entry Zone:

■ How to Draw an Entry Zone?

- To draw an entry zone at the resistance level, draw a box from the high to low of the last red candle of Move 1 of an downward move (for resistance); and

- To draw an entry zone at the support level, draw a box from the high to low of the last green candle of an upward move (for support)

- In simple words, an entry zone on is always every highest body green candle of an upward move and an entry zone is always every lowest body red candle of a downward move.

- See example below:

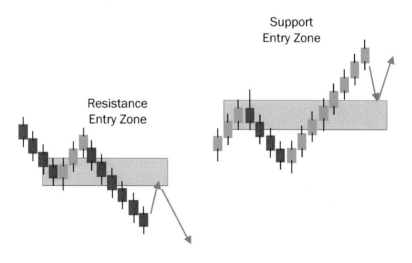

Support
Entry Zone

Resistance
Entry Zone

https://www.youtube.com/@TraderRiaz

Entry Zone:

■ **Example of an Entry Zone on Chart:**

- The below example is of a downtrend, in which you can see that the last red candle of Move 1 of this downtrend becomes our entry zone.

- When price breaks and closes below this Move 1, we mark this red candle as our entry zone.

- We plan our entry once price retests this zone.

Entry Reasons:

- You have successfully learned that how to find trend? How to find perfect support and resistance levels? And how to make perfect entry zones at your support or resistance levels to plan your next entry position.

- Considering the price reaches your entry zone, now this is the time to look for the possible entry reasons.

- There are numerous entry reasons to look for while price is in your entry zone but we will learn only the most frequently appeared entry reasons on the chart.

- Because I believe less but concrete knowledge can bring you better results instead of flooding your mind with dozens of entry setups.

- Let's start learning our entry reasons in the coming slides.

Candlesticks:

■ How to Read a Candlestick Behavior?

■ Important Candlestick Patterns

– Bullish / Bearish Engulfing Candle

– Hammer / Pinbar Candle / Hanging Man Candle

– Shooting Star / Inverted Hammer Candle

– Spinning Top Candle

– Inside Bar Candle

Candlesticks:

■ How to Read a Candlestick Behavior?

- Every candle has its own story. You just need to understand what actually candle is trying to tell you. If you are able to understand the candlestick behavior, you will be able to make quick and accurate trading decisions accordingly.

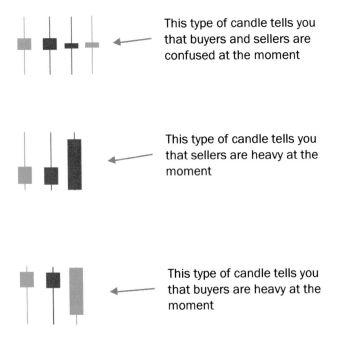

This type of candle tells you that buyers and sellers are confused at the moment

This type of candle tells you that sellers are heavy at the moment

This type of candle tells you that buyers are heavy at the moment

Important Candlesticks:

■ Engulfing Candlestick Patterns:

- Whenever you find a bullish engulfing candle on support level, it shows you an immense buyers pressure and provides an opportunity to open your BUY / LONG trade.

- Whenever you find a bearish engulfing candle on resistance level, it shows you an immense sellers pressure and provides an opportunity to open your SELL / SHORT trade.

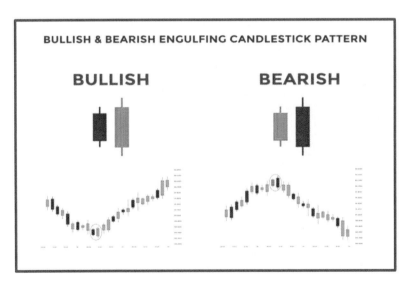

BULLISH & BEARISH ENGULFING CANDLESTICK PATTERN

BULLISH   **BEARISH**

Important Candlesticks:

■ Hammer / Pinbar / Hanging Man Candle:

- Whenever you find a hammer candle, a pinbar candle or a hanging man candle on support or resistance level, it provides you the reversal trading opportunity.

- This type of candle on support or resistance shows that the current trend has lost its momentum and we might have a reversal soon.

- The body & top wick of this candle must fit in the 38.2% of the fib level to be qualified as a perfect hammer, pinbar or hammer candle.

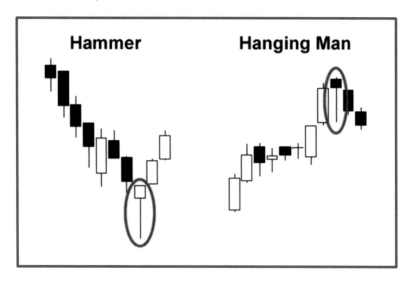

Important Candlesticks:

■ Inverted Hammer / Shooting Star Candle:

- Whenever you find a shooting star or inverted hammer candle on support or resistance level, it provides you the reversal trading opportunity.

- This type of candle on support or resistance shows that the current trend has lost its momentum and we might have a reversal soon.

- The body & bottom wick of this candle must fit in the 38.2% of the fib level to be qualified as a perfect shooting star or inverted hammer candle.

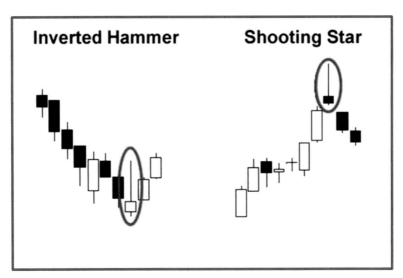

Important Candlesticks:

■ Spinning Top Candle:

- Whenever you find a spinning top candle on support or resistance level, just wait for the breakout of its low or high (depending on the situation) and place your trade accordingly.

- The candle should have a small body at around center of the whole candle. But it has a variety of shapes as shown in the picture.

- This is a reversal trading setup.

- This type of candle on support or resistance shows that the current trend has lost its momentum and we might have a reversal soon.

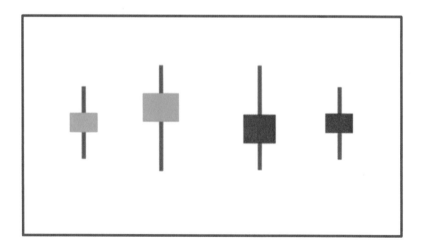

https://www.youtube.com/@TraderRiaz

Important Candlesticks:

■ Inside Bar Candle:

– Whenever you find an inside bar candlestick pattern on support or resistance level, just wait for the breakout of the low or high (depending on the situation) of the second candle (which is actually the inside bar) and then place your trade accordingly.

– The 2nd candle must be fully covered by the previous candle (which is named as Mother Candle) as shown in the picture.

– This is a reversal trading setup.

– This type of candle on support or resistance shows that the current trend has lost its momentum and we might have a reversal soon.

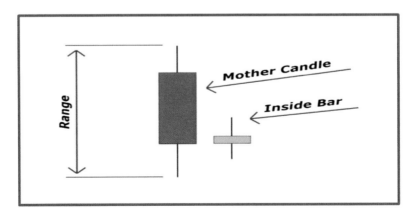

Chart Patterns:

- Important Chart Patterns
  - Double Top
  - Double Bottom

Chart Patterns:

■ Double Top:

- A double top has an 'M' shape and indicates a bearish reversal in trend.

  - ■ You have to open sell trade on double top only if you find this chart pattern on a resistance level.

  - ■ Entry Setup 1 (Aggressive Entry):

    - You can open your trade on the second top as soon as you get any rejection candle (a red candle) and place stop loss above the highest wick of double top.

  - ■ Entry Setup 2 (Conventional Entry):

    - You can open your trade on the breakout and retest of the neckline and place stop loss above the neckline zone.

- This type of chart pattern on resistance levels shows that the current uptrend has lost its momentum and we might have a reversal soon.

- For reference please watch this video:
  https://youtu.be/Lhqvgme5W14

Chart Patterns:

■ **Double Top:**

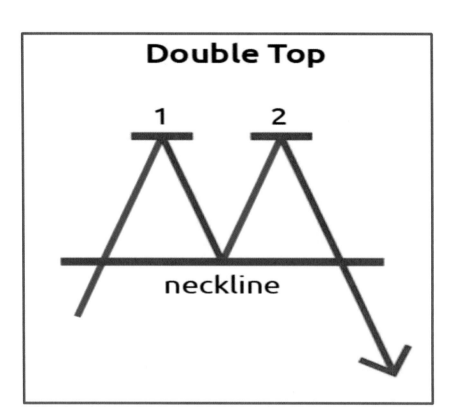

Chart Patterns:

■ Double Top Rules:

– Draw a box from the highest wick to the highest body of the first top to make a termination zone.

– Any candle of the second top cannot close above this termination zone box.

– If any candle of the second top closes above the box, then the double top becomes invalid.

– There must be minimum two candles from the 1st top to neckline and minimum two candles from the neckline to 2nd top.

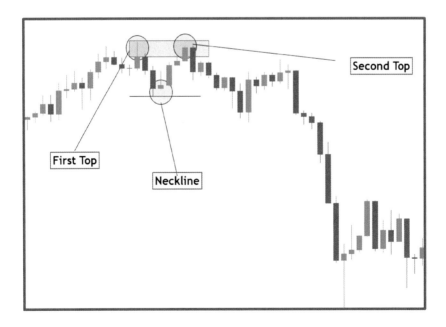

Chart Patterns:

■ Double Bottom:

- A double top has an 'W' shape and indicates a bullish reversal in trend.

  - ■ You have to open buy trade on double bottom only if you find this chart pattern on a support level.

  - ■ Entry Setup 1 (Aggressive Entry):

    - You can open your trade on the second bottom as soon as you get any rejection candle (a green candle) and place stop loss below the lowest wick of double bottom.

  - ■ Entry Setup 2 (Conventional Entry):

    - You can open your trade on the breakout and retest of the neckline and place stop loss below the neckline zone.

- This type of chart pattern on support levels shows that the current downtrend has lost its momentum and we might have a reversal soon.

- For reference please watch this video:

  https://youtu.be/Lhqvgme5W14

Chart Patterns:

■ Double Bottom:

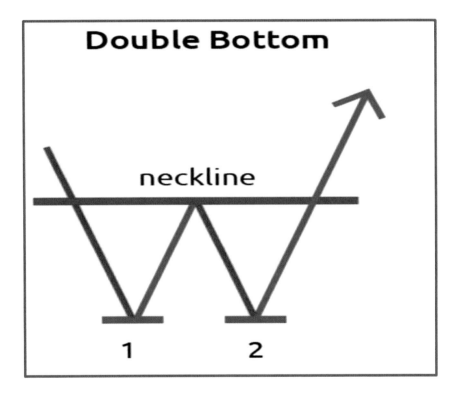

Chart Patterns:

■ Double Bottom Rules:

- Draw a box from the lowest wick to the lowest body of the first bottom to make a termination zone.

- Any candle of the second bottom cannot close below this termination zone box.

- If any candle of the second bottom closes below the box, then the double bottom becomes invalid.

- There must be minimum two candles from the 1st bottom to neckline and minimum two candles from the neckline to 2nd bottom.

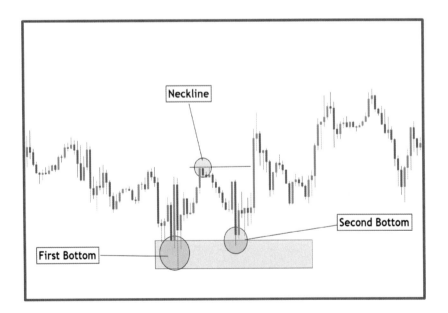

My Trading Strategy:

- Step 1:

  - Find Trend

- Step 2:

  - Find Support or Resistance Level

- Step 3:

  - Don't rush, wait for the price to come back to your defined support or resistance level.

  - Once the price is there, find any of the above mentioned entry reasons.

  - If you find your entry reason then don't think too much, don't get involved into over analysis and just hit the BUY / SELL button and leave the rest on the market.

Day Trading Setup:

- **Step 1:**

  - Find trend in 15 minutes time frame

- **Step 2:**

  - Find support or resistance level in 15 minutes time frame

  - Draw your entry zone on the support or resistance levels as you just learned in previous slides

- **Step 3:**

  - Don't rush, wait for the price to come back to your defined entry zone.

  - Once the price is there, drop down to 1 minute time frame to find any of the above mentioned entry reasons.

  - If you find your entry reason then don't think too much, don't get involved into over analysis and just hit the BUY / SELL button and leave the rest on the market.

Swing Trading Setup:

- Step 1:

  - Find trend in 4 hours time frame

- Step 2:

  - Find support or resistance level in 4 hours time frame

  - Draw your entry zone on the support or resistance levels as you just learned in previous slides

- Step 3:

  - Don't rush, wait for the price to come back to your defined entry zone.

  - Once the price is there, drop down to 5 minutes or 15 minutes time frame to find any of the above mentioned entry reasons.

  - If you find your entry reason then don't think too much, don't get involved into over analysis and just hit the BUY / SELL button and leave the rest on the market.

Our Trading Strategy:

■ **Useful Tips:**

- Don't change your trading strategy often.

- Always stay consistent to your trading strategy.

- Never go for a second trading strategy unless you place at least 100 trades to prove your strategy is not working.

- If you are getting above 50 percent positive trades on your trading strategy, it means your strategy is good. You just need to fine tune it to bring better results.

- Any strategy that gives 55 to 70 percent winning trades, is considered excellent trading strategy.

- Never open your trade without STOP LOSS. Just stick to your STOP LOSS and do not extend it at all.

- Never close your trade before your targeted TAKE PROFIT area.

- For a longer term consistent profit, your trade should be opened with 1 to 1.4 Risk to Reward Ratio.

- You must use ATR indicator to calculate your STOP LOSS. Watch this video for reference:

  https://youtu.be/XSf7cXCZ7go

Our Trading Strategy:

■ Useful Tips:

    – You can easily find ATR indicator on www.tradingview.com even in free account.

    – Hover the mouse over the candle that gives you the entry reason and you can use (2 x ATR) as your STOP LOSS but you can refine this STOP LOSS according to your research.

    – For example if ATR is 35 pips then your STOP LOSS should be 35 x 2 = 70 pips.

    – I use ATR indicator with default setting but you can adjust it according to your own research.

Trade Management:

- **Buy Trade:**

    - Suppose you open your BUY position and the price just crosses the nearest swing high. Immediately trail your STOP LOSS to breakeven.

    - Move your stop loss below of every upcoming structure as soon as the price breaks and closes above that structure level.

    - You can take your targe price area to nearest upcoming resistance level.

- **Sell Trade:**

    - Suppose you open your SELL position and the price just crosses the nearest swing low. Immediately trail your STOP LOSS to breakeven.

    - Move your stop loss above of every upcoming structure as soon as the price breaks and closes below that structure level.

    - You can take your target price area to nearest upcoming support level.

Risk Management:

■ You can't become a successful trader if you don't know how to manage risk:

  – First of all divide your equity by 100.

  – Suppose you have $1000 as your trading balance, divide it with 100, it results in $10 in this case ($1000 / 10 = $100)

  – This $10 now becomes the maximum STOP LOSS amount you can set for a single trade, which actually is 1% of your total account balance

  – Never put more than $10 in a single trade if you have $1000 account balance. It will allow you to lose 100 trades in a row before blowing your account, and it can't happen that you lose 100 trades in a row.

  – Never open more than 5 trades simultaneously.

  – Never throw above 6% of the total account balance in the market as STOP LOSS. It means your maximum draw down at a time must not exceed 6% of your total account balance.

  – For reference watch this video: https://youtu.be/Ot2tzBcEA8U

RSI Divergence:

- RSI Divergence Trading Strategy is my personal favorite trading strategy. It really works exceptionally well especially if you find it on any support or resistance level.

- There are two major types of RSI Divergences
  - Regular RSI Divergence:
    - Regular RSI divergence provides trend reversal trading opportunity.
    - There are two types of regular RSI divergences:
      - Regular Bullish Divergence
      - Regular Bearish Divergence
  - Hidden RSI Divergence:
    - Hidden RSI divergence provides trend continuation trading opportunity.
    - There are two types of hidden RSI divergences:
      - Hidden Bullish Divergence
      - Hidden Bearish Divergence

RSI Divergence:

■ Regular RSI Divergence:

   – Regular Bullish Divergence:

     ■ Regular bullish divergence forms when price is making new lower low but RSI is showing new higher low as shown in the picture.

     ■ Your are safe to place buy trade afterwards.

RSI Divergence:

- Regular RSI Divergence:

  - Regular Bearish Divergence:

    - Regular bearish divergence forms when price is making new higher high but RSI is showing new lower high as shown in the picture.

    - You are safe to place sell trade afterwards.

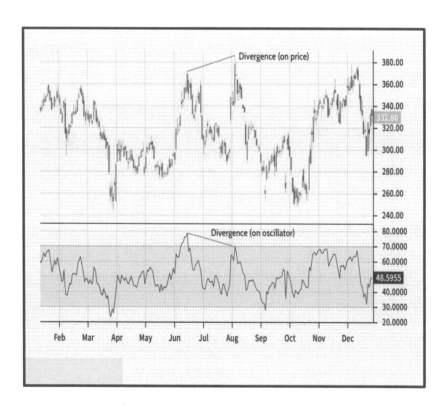

RSI Divergence:

- Hidden RSI Divergence:
  - Hidden Bullish Divergence:
    - Hidden bullish divergence forms when price is making new higher low but RSI is showing new lower low as shown in the picture.
    - Your are safe to place buy trade afterwards.

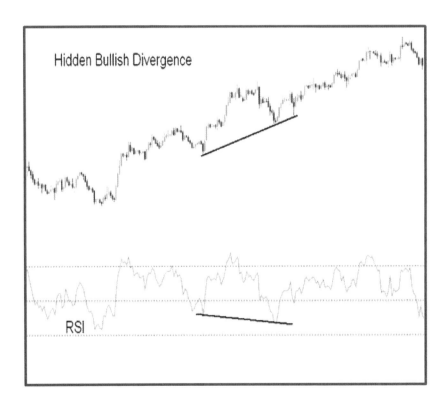

RSI Divergence:

- Hidden RSI Divergence:

  - Hidden Bearish Divergence:

    - Hidden bearish divergence forms when price is making new lower high but RSI is showing new higher high as shown in the picture.

    - Your are safe to place sell trade afterwards.

Hidden Bearish Divergence

Riaz Academy:

- **Address:**
  - Office No. 151-A, 2nd Floor, Sector C, Commercial Zone, Bahria Town, Lahore, Punjab, Pakistan.

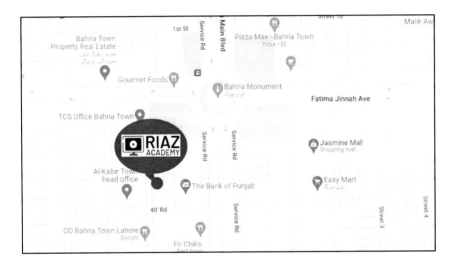

- **WhatsApp Helpline:**
  - 001 (234) 546-7272

  https://www.facebook.com/TradeRriaz

  https://www.twitter.com/TradeRriaz

  https://www.instagram.com/TradeRriazOfficial

  https://www.youtube.com/@TradeRriaz

Made in the USA
Middletown, DE
30 September 2023